To Masali

"LAYING ASIDE EVERY WEIGHT"
(Far Beyond What You Eat)

Evangelist Tiffany Breon and Bishop Ray Neal

Thanks for your support!.

Blessings

Evangelist
Tiffany Breon

E. Bishop Ray Neal

Bishop Ray Neal

First Printing: 2018

ISBN 978-0-359-03822-0

Tiffany Breon Ministries
tbreon@yahoo.com

Acknowledgements

I would like to thank my pastor Bishop Ray Neal for his encouragement, wisdom and contributions to this project. I would also like to thank my confidant and prayer partner Danise Johnson for helping to format and edit the final draft of this project. Last but certainly not least, I would like to thank my parents and the Ferguson 5 for their continued support.

Blessings and love to each of you….

Tiffany Breon

Contents

Introduction

Hebrew: 12:1(KJV)
Wherefore seeing we also are compassed about with so great a cloud of witnesses, let us lay aside every weight, and the sin which doth so easily beset us, and let us run with patience the race that is set before us.

As we walk through this journey that we call life over a period of time we develop mindsets, habits, behaviors, and relationships that are instrumental in shaping us into the people that we are. It is through these multiple life experiences that we accumulate excessive "weights"… In the natural sense, weights are instrumental in helping us to build our physical stamina. In our quest to build our spiritual stamina, it is vitally important that we take notice of how carrying negative spiritual weights can potentially cause us to miss out on the blessings of God.

What is a weight?

The Dictionary defines **weight** as, a mental or moral burden, as of care, sorrow or responsibility. Each day poses new opportunities and challenges, yet it is up to us to determine how we will handle every situation. Have you ever found yourself worrying about something that was beyond your control and when all was said and done, things seemed to just work out despite how overwhelmed you may have felt?

When we allow the cares of life to weigh on us and, when we ignore the leading of the Holy Spirit, we will eventually find ourselves in a place of stagnation, unable to move forward in the things of God.

Living on Purpose

It has never been the will of God for us as His creation to live without fulfilling our God given purposes on earth yet there are many people who have aborted their assignments due to disobedience. The most unfortunate thing is when we ignore the silent self-destructive behaviors that pose a threat to our kingdom assignments, we sadly discover that we have wasted a lot of valuable time. For many years, we have searched outwardly to find the answer to humanity's question," How do we find happiness and fulfillment in life?" The truth of the matter is the greatest fulfillment in life comes from discovering our God given purpose and walking in it. Over the years, many of us have encountered circumstances and situations that have caused us to be emotionally traumatized yet instead of confronting the real issues behind the trauma and the damage they've caused, we subconsciously or even consciously dismiss them, never acknowledging their existence.

Until we begin to deal with the root of the matter and release what has happened, we cannot embrace the beauty of what's in store for us. The one thing that God wants us to realize is that our life experiences are merely pieces of a puzzle that He has allowed to come together to make us the masterpieces that we truly are. As God's masterful creation, it's time for us to take a true stand for Jesus Christ as it relates to the healing and edification (build up, restore, promote growth) of the universal body of Christ as a whole. No longer can we allow our circumstances to dictate to us. We as a people have got to exercise our kingdom authority over every demonic force that has hindered us from operating as kingdom custodians. Passivity will not do, it's time to pursue and overtake with spiritual force.

What We Don't Know Can Hurt Us
Have you ever gone through something that was painful only to discover that if you had known what the outcome would have been, you would have made a different choice? Many of us have had to face the harsh reality of dealing with circumstances that produced an unexpected outcome. It is important that we make a concerted effort to educate ourselves in areas where we lack understanding. Our awareness in different areas of our lives will determine what we accomplish in life.

As we move forward in our God given purpose, we must do our best to choose wisely.

(Hosea 4:6a) My people are destroyed for a lack of knowledge:

One of the greatest downfalls for many of us is our lack of knowledge as it relates to proper decision making. As you read this book, it is our sincere desire that each and every reader will not only be enlightened to a greater revelation of God's will and purpose for their individual lives, but it is also our desire and prayer that by reading this book, other believers in Christ will see the importance of releasing any physical and emotional baggage that has restricted their movement. Anything that attributes to our spiritual deprivation can potentially cause us to function beneath our kingdom potential. It's time to deal with all internal and external hindrances that we may run the race that is set before us. It's time to lose weight!!!

Chapter 1
"The Spirit of Fear (The Silent Thief)"

Though its effects are not always visible, fear has paralyzed the hearts and minds of men and women everywhere. In order to receive deliverance from the Spirit of fear, we must be willing to admit that there is a problem. When we understand the severity of the effects of fear, we must take the necessary steps towards addressing the root of the matter. Fear has the ability to bring about unnecessary stress and worry and it can affect our daily activities. When under the influence of fear, emotional instability and spiritual stagnation are inevitable.

What is fear?

Fear is a distressing emotion aroused by impending danger, evil, pain etc. Whether real or imagined, fear is the feeling or condition of being afraid. The spirit of fear has a way of blinding us and it reveals our inability to trust God as our protector and provider.

Have you ever had to speak in front of a group of strangers and as you stood to speak, your heart began to beat rapidly? Though there may not have been anything to justify your anxiety, no matter who you are, no matter how old or young you are, each of us has dealt with fear to some degree.

While most would not acknowledge fear as being a personal heart issue, we can't ignore the fact that fear of the unknown, fear of failure, fear of loneliness, fear of success, fear of not living up to the expectations of self and others have all played a part in hindering us from moving forward.

"Whatever is at the root Will Manifest as Fruit"

When we fail to deal with the root cause of fear, it will eventually manifest as the fruit of doubt, irritability and worry. When these three emotions are in operation, the end result is spiritual paralysis.

What does it mean to be paralyzed?

The word **paralyzed** is defined as a place of hopeless stoppage, inactivity, or inability to act.

Spiritual paralysis is one of the greatest indications that the spirit of fear has taken control. Allowing fear to lead or control us is a choice. When we come to the awareness of the effects of fear, it is up to us to make every effort to deal with the root cause of it. We must be ever mindful of the fact that we have the ability to determine what spirits are granted access into our lives.

"Understanding Fear as written in the word of God"

There is a distinct difference between the spirit of fear and having a reverential fear of God. In order to be delivered from the spirit of fear, we must acknowledge that it does exist, and we must know that the spirit of fear did not come from God. When speaking in terms of good fear, many would ask how can anything good possibly come from fear? Glad you asked…

Proverbs 1:7 (a) says, "The fear of the Lord is the beginning of knowledge…" **(KJV)**

2 Timothy 1:7 says, "For God has not given us the spirit of fear but of power and of love and of sound mind." **(KJV)**

At first glance, it may appear that the word fear is used in the same context. It is with that thought in mind that we see the need to venture further.

When we look at **Proverbs 1:7 (a)** The fear of the Lord is the beginning of knowledge.
We see that in this context, the writer uses the term **theosebia** which is the Greek term for fear, meaning reverence for God or fear of God (Strong's Concordance).

However, when we look at **2 Timothy 1:7** For God has not given us the spirit of fear but of power and of love and of sound mind, we see that in this context, the writer uses the term **deilia** which is the Greek term for fear meaning cowardice which is the translation for fearful, timid or afraid (Strong's Concordance).

"The Results of Fear"

In this section, the type of fear that we want to focus on is fear (deilia) which brings negative results.

2 Timothy 1:7 For God has not given us the spirit of fear but of power and of love and of sound mind.

When we are consumed with fear, it affects three critical areas of our lives; Our physical and mental strength, our ability to embrace authentic relationships, and our ability to see clearly.

Unfruitfulness

Have you ever invested time and energy into unhealthy activities or relationships out of fear and entered into a difficult trial as a result of that decision? Have you ever felt like the trial that you were experiencing lasted far too long, so much so that it made you feel like you exhausted all of your natural strength? In relation to our physical and mental strength, investing time and energy in relationships and activities that are unfruitful out of fear oftentimes opens the door to anger, resentment and emotional fatigue.

The dictionary defines the word **unfruitful** as, not providing satisfaction, unprofitable. In other words, it means to not bear fruit; it is fruitless or barren.

Example – An Unfruitful Tree

It is with this thought in mind that we are reminded of the story where Jesus cursed the fig tree in (**Mark 11 verses 12 – 14**). After seeing a fig tree from a distance with leaves on it, Jesus became excited because he was hungry, the tree had leaves so perhaps it would have fruit. After reaching the tree, Jesus discovered that there were leaves but no fruit. In response, Jesus cursed the fig tree by saying that no one would ever eat from it again and it did not bear fruit from that day forward. On that day, the tree withered from the roots and died. **(Emphasis added)**
This story is a prime example of how we should govern our daily lives. When we encounter people and situations that are not producing fruit that is in keeping with our kingdom assignment we must determine if their barrenness has the ability to cause us to abort the dreams and visions that God placed in our hearts.

In relation to our power, when we invest time and energy in relationships that cause us to feel grieved and depleted of our strength, and when we participate in activities that are not in alignment with our assignments, mental and emotional fatigue will set in and we cannot bear the fruit that God expects. In no way are we suggesting that because those relationships are unfruitful that we are to curse (doom) others or ourselves with our words. What we are saying is that we must have faith in God, believing that what we say will come to pass, using our words in ways that manifest the power of the Kingdom of God in our lives and the lives of others so that we will bear fruit. We must always be prayerful, of our associations and we must also have enough discernment to know when to walk away from relationships and situations that are toxic. Sometimes, it's just not the season although at first glance it appears to be.

Seeing and Thinking Clearly

Fear has the ability to blind us from seeing the sincerity of the hearts of mankind. When we have spiritual blinders on, it affects our ability to embrace authentic relationships. There have been times in each of our lives where we have felt betrayed and rejected by people that were close to us. In most instances, we become traumatized as a result of our failure to understand that all human beings have the ability to potentially hurt us no matter what roles they play in our lives. When we choose to dwell on our past hurts, it is impossible to move forward. Because of our lack of trust, we tend look at everyone as a threat or enemy, always questioning their motives and we end up losing out on good relationships and opportunities.

The last area that fear of affects is our ability to think clearly. Thoughts rooted in fear are unhealthy. When we allow unhealthy thoughts to linger, it affects our ability to make sound decisions. One minute we're in, next minute we're out. Indecisiveness will always breed confusion in our lives if we allow it to persist.
Maintaining our focus is absolutely necessary if we want to see the natural manifestation of what God has for us.

James 1:8 (KJV) A double minded man is unstable in all his ways.

The dictionary says to be **double minded** is to be two souled, wavering or undecided in mind.
In **Matthew 14: 22 – 31 (KJV),** the very moment Peter took his focus off Jesus and began to doubt, he started to sink.
If we are to operate with singleness of mind, we

must determine within ourselves, no matter what it looks like, no matter what it feels like, we are going to keep our minds focused on Jesus. When we keep our minds on Jesus, He will give us continual peace that is beyond our comprehension. When it comes to dealing with the cares of life, we cannot do it on our own. God has given each of us a special grace that empowers us to do the things we were anointed to do. He gives us the ability to love the unlovable with the love of God, and he gives us soundness of mind as spoken of in **Philippians 4:7(KJV)** And the peace of God which passeth all understanding, shall keep your hearts and minds through Christ Jesus".

Questions

1. Pray and ask God to reveal areas in which you struggle with fear. What did He reveal?

2. Name five areas that you know that fear has robbed you of your inheritance as a believer in Christ.

3. In what ways has your life been stagnant due to fear?

4. How is the fear of the Lord different from a spirit of fear?

5. Name three unfruitful situations or relationships that you have been in and are currently in. What fruit are you not bearing as a result of investing your time and energy into those situations? Pray for Godly wisdom and direction. Write down three scriptural promises from God pertaining those matters and confess them.

6. In what ways has fear caused you to miss out on authentic, healthy relationships or caused you to operate in fear and/or suspicion towards others?

7. Name a few thoughts rooted in fear that are holding you back. In what ways is doublemindedness manifesting in your life because of it? Pray and petition to God regarding these matters, reject the lies and embrace the truth of God's word. Receive the peace of God

8. Pray to the Father, renounce ungodly fear and receive the blessing of healthy fear, the fear of the Lord which is the beginning of wisdom.

Keys to overcoming our fears

1. **We must identify the areas where we allowed the spirit fear to creep in.**

2 Corinthians 2:11 Lest Satan should get an advantage of us: We are not to be ignorant of his devices.

The dictionary defines the word device as, a plan or scheme to affect purpose.

When we fall prey to the spirit of fear, we are ultimately tricking ourselves into embracing self-defeating thoughts that keep us in a place of bondage. Our knowledge of the word of God is our greatest defense against the mind binding attacks of the enemy.

2. **We must earnestly seek the heart of God concerning our fears, casting our every care upon Him.**

Peter 5:7 (KJV) Casting all your cares upon Him for He cares for you.

The dictionary says to **cast,** is to throw off or away. To part with or lose, to shed or drop. As we release the weight of all we have tried to carry on our own, we clear the path for what God has in store for us.

3. We must trust that while where we are weak, God is our strength.

2. Corinthians 12: 9 (a) (KJV) And he said unto me, my grace is sufficient for thee: for my strength is made perfect in weakness…

When God perfects His strength in us, the results are undeniable. **The Dictionary** defines the word **perfect** as, entirely without flaws, defects, or short comings. It means to be accurate, exact or correct in every detail. When we move and act in the perfect strength of God, even our naysayers will pause and say, surely the Lord is with us.

Chapter 2
"What is Hidden Has the Ability to Hinder"

Oftentimes we have heard that we can't judge something by appearance alone. Lurking beneath the physical shells of men and women everywhere are the hidden contaminates of the human heart. From day to day we put on our external masks in hope that no one sees the real us. The most saddening thing is, in putting on our masks we spiral into a place of personal denial which leads to unaddressed heart issues.

Psalms 51:10 (KJV) create in me a clean and renew a right spirit within me.

When we look at the 10th verse of Psalms 51, David is making an appeal to God asking Him to create in him a clean heart and renew a right spirit within him. After being confronted by the prophet Nathan concerning his sinful behavior, David realized the error of his way. This particular verse was written as a result of David's adulterous affair with Bathsheba which gives us a clear example of how sinful behavior can lead to a web of deception **(See 2 Samuel Chapters 11 and 12).**

In many instances dealing with our own personal heart issues can be difficult. It is of great necessity that each of us comes to a place of brokenness and repentance that our hearts might be cleansed of all potential contaminates.

When something is **contaminated**, it is impure, unsuitable by contrast or mixture with something unclean or bad.

While some contaminates are seen with the natural eye, the most dangerous contaminates are the ones that are deeply rooted in our hearts such as bitterness, un-forgiveness, jealousy, hatred, criticism, etc. When our hearts are contaminated, we spend our lives viewing things through the tinted lenses of our personal experiences. Have you ever been in a relationship and something the other person said or did triggered a negative response based on something you experienced in the past? If the answer is yes, chances are there are hidden contaminates that need to be cleansed from your heart. When something is **clean**, it is free from dirt, it is unsoiled, unstained and free from foreign matter. As we compare the natural to the spiritual, foreign matter can be anything that we harbor in our hearts that is not in keeping with the word of God. Contaminates of the hearts can hinder our prayers from being answered.

Psalms 66: 18 (KJV) if I regard iniquity in my heart, the Lord will not hear me.

In many instances, when there is a delay in having our prayers answered, weariness, anger, depression and, frustration tend to set in. When these emotions are in operation, they can potentially cause strained relationships, health issues, and it can cause our spiritual senses to be dull, clouding our ability to see clearly.

The more we ignore the hidden contaminates of our hearts, the more susceptible we are to placing ourselves in a position of stagnation.

Stagnation – failure to progress or advance, having stopped as ceasing to run or flow.

Prolonged periods of stagnation are one of the many tricks that the enemy uses in an attempt to keep us mentally and emotionally oppressed. While the word of God uses the word heart and mind interchangeably, when speaking of the mind in this context we are talking about the seat of the emotions which include the mind, the will, the emotions, the reason and intellect of man. As we are enlightened to a greater understanding the benefits of a clean heart, it is our responsibility to share our revelation with others that there might be more light!!!

Questions

1. Ask God to reveal hidden contaminates in your heart. What did He reveal? Pray Psalms 51:10 over yourself.

2. How have they affected your life thus far?

3. Name the ways these contaminants have caused you to be stagnant.
<u>Key Requirements for Cleansing and Maintaining a Clean Heart</u>

1. We must be willing to forgive daily not allowing offenses to linger.

Matthew 6:14 if you forgive men their trespasses your Heavenly Father will also forgive you.

2. We must have at least one person that we are accountable to; someone who will tell us the truth even when we don't want to hear it.

Proverbs 11:14 (KJV) says, Where no counsel is people fall: but in the multitude of counsellors there is safety.

3. We must guard our hearts against people and things that would cause us to indulge in sinful behavior.

Proverbs 4:23 (KJV) Keep thy heart with all diligence; for out of it are the issues of life.

(NLT) says, Guard your heart above all else for it determines the course of your life.

To guard means to keep safe from harm or danger. To take precautions, to give protection. When the heart is left unprotected and in a contaminated state, we place ourselves in danger of missing the course/path that God has predestined for us.

Chapter 3

"Avoiding the Pitfalls of Wrong Choices"

Daily, from sun up to sun down, we have to make choices in some form or another. While some choices are not as detrimental as others, over the course of time we discover that one choice can affect our lives and the lives of the people that are connected to us. It is imperative that we pay close attention to the voice and motivation behind our decision making. It is the power of choice that determines the path that we will travel in our pursuit to fulfilling our destiny. **Genesis Chapter 16** describes how making a wrong choice in efforts to see the fulfillment of God's promise to bless the descendants of Abraham can lead to disaster. After having waited for Gods promise for 10 years without seeing the manifestation, Sarah encouraged her husband Abraham to lay with her servant Hagar because they felt that they were too old to conceive. After Hagar did conceive giving birth to a son which was named Ishmael, Sarah became jealous because she didn't fully consider the emotional trauma that her decision would birth. **(Emphasis added See Genesis 16).** No matter how much knowledge we acquire, as long as we live, no one is exempt from making wrong choices.

In many instances, our wrong choices are a direct result of allowing our emotions to lead as opposed to following the leading of the Holy Spirit.
John 16:13 (KJV) Howbeit when He, the Spirit of Truth, is come, He will guide you into all truth: for He shall not speak of himself; but whatsoever he shall hear, that shall he speak: and he will show you things to come.

The Holy Spirit is the internal compass that God has given to each of us to direct us in the way that we should go. Therefore, we must watch as well as pray in an effort to avoid the pitfalls of wrong choices. A **pitfall** is defined as a lightly covered and unnoticeable pit prepared as a trap for people or animals. From a spiritual perspective, in life we will encounter people, places and, things that are designed to trap us.

"The consequences of wrong Choices"

It is of utmost importance that we take notice of the pitfalls that come disguised in ways that are appealing to the appetite of our souls. Have you ever made a decision that you knew wasn't right, yet you ignored that still small voice and proceeded to move forward? Ignoring that still small voice over time, leads to dullness of hearing in the spirit.

Our God is a gentleman and because of that, He will not superimpose His will upon us. When we do things as an act of our own will, we end up out of the ark of safety, sadly having to experience the consequences of our wrong choices. When God has spoken a word over our lives, our obedience to His directives and patience is absolutely imperative. In many cases, being patient isn't easy, but the benefits are of great value.

Patience- is the ability or willingness to suppress restlessness or annoyance when confronted with delay.

James 1:3 (KJV) Knowing this, that the trying of your faith worketh patience.

In this verse, the word patience is referring to our level of maturity. When we come to a place of spiritual maturity and, we learn the art of obedience, we are more apt to make decisions that lead us to the path that God ordained specifically for us. The word of God tells of how it took Noah about 100 years to build the ark. Surely there were people that laughed at him because of the amount of time it took. Noah took heed to the specific details that God had given even though he was surrounded by disobedience. Through diligence, patience and obedience, God allowed Noah and his family replenished the earth after the destructive flood. **(See Genesis 6 through 9).**

Questions

1. Have you ever made a wrong choice because you didn't believe God was going to do what he promised you? If so, what was the choice and what was the promise?

2. What are some of the pitfalls that you've fallen in or been tempted to fall in due to a desire in your soul?

3. Are there promises that seem to be taking a long time that have not come to pass? Write them down and pray for patience.

4. Name a few ways that impatience caused you to disobey the Holy Spirit's instructions?

Ways to avoid the pitfall of Wrong Choices

1. We must trust God when we don't understand

Proverbs 3:5-6 (KJV) Trust in the Lord with all thine heart; and lean not to thine own understanding. In all thy ways acknowledge Him and He shall direct thy paths.

2. We must Obey Gods instructions as written in the word of God.

Joshua 1:8 (KJV) This book of the law shall not depart out of thy mouth; but thou shall meditate therein day and night, that thou mayest observe to do all that is written therein: for then thou shall make thy way prosperous and thou shalt have good success.

3. We must ask God to direct our steps.

Psalms 37:23 (KJV) the steps of a good man are ordered by the Lord, and He delights in his way.

Chapter 4
"Removing all Doubt and Renewing Our Mind"

Romans 12: 2 (KJV) and be not conformed to this world but be ye transformed by the renewing of your mind, that ye may prove what is that good, and acceptable and perfect, will of God.

One of the greatest lessons that any of us could ever learn is how to conquer the demons of our own minds. Most of us spend the majority of our time talking about how busy the enemy is, yet we fail to realize that our most ignored enemies are the thoughts that we replay in our minds. It is through the mind binding powers of the enemy that we fall prey to self-destructive behaviors. When we began to dwell on the lies of the enemy, accepting things that are in direct opposition of the word of God, spiritual oppression is inevitable. **Oppression means,** to be burdened down with cruel or unjust impositions or restraints. It is to lie heavily on the mind as sleep or weariness does.

God Wants Our Full Attention!!!

When we focus our attention on the cares of life such as financial issues, health problems, drama on the job, relationship issues, rebellious children, loss of a loved one.... Our attitude during these times can cause us to become discouraged.

Philippians 4:8 (KJV) Finally, bretheren whatsoever things are true, whatsoever things are honest, whatsoever things are just, whatsoever things are pure, whatsoever things are lovely, whatsoever things are of good report; if there be any virtue, and if there be any praise, think on these things.

Change Becomes Change When We Change (Our thinking and our confessions go hand and hand.)

Change is to make different, to altar, to transform, or replace with another

Our perspective in life will generally affect our outcome. When we see things from a **pessimistic** perspective, our outlook is gloomy or negative. Pessimistic attitudes are fueled by doubt, wrong thinking and wrong confessions. When we make confessions that are not in alignment with the word and will of God, we create and frame an environment that limits our ability to thrive in a positive manner. Have you ever spoken something negative out of your mouth and it actually happened? It was through the creative power of words that God created the world. We are God's master creation, created in His likeness and image, therefore we have the ability to create what we want to see manifest whether good or bad. Words have

power… God always wants what's best for us, but we must make a concerted effort to do our parts.
3 John 2 (KJV) Beloved, I wish above all things that thou mayest prosper and be in health, even as thy soul prospereth.

In order to have a prosperous soul, we must truly come to know the will of the Father as written in the word of God. If there is any area of our lives that is not reflective of what the word of God says concerning us, it is a liar and thief.

John 10:10 the thief comes only to steal to kill and destroy; I have come that they may have life, and have it to the full.

Full – completely filled, containing all that can be held; filled to the utmost capacity. Abundant; well-supplied.

God intended for us to live abundant lives, yet until transformation has taken place, we will continue to live our lives accepting less than His best.
Let's look at the second verse of **Romans 12 in the King James Version,** which reads, And be not conformed to this world: but be ye **transformed** by the **renewing** of your mind, that ye may prove what is that good, and acceptable, and perfect, will of God.

In this context, the word world is referring to the "age" or "era" which is referring to a specific point in time. It is not the will of the Father for the world to dictate to the body of Christ how to live. As the body, it is far past time for us to stand and take our position as kingdom representatives. When true transformation takes place, we change in form, appearance, or structure; metamorphose.

The word **transformation** in the Greek is **metamorphoo**, which comes from the word **metamorphosis** – which means to change into another form.

Our transformation is necessary if we as believers are going to operate in the same power and authority that Jesus did. It's time for us to take the kingdom by force. We can't keep sitting on the sidelines of passivity allowing ourselves to be so distracted with our own problems that we fail to see the needs of others. We can't keep yielding to the desires of our flesh, abusing the grace card, giving our power to demons for a few minutes of pleasure not concerned about the sin that's keeping us separated from God. When we are transformed, we refuse to accept generational curses; we refuse to accept sickness, disease and premature deaths. We refuse to live from paycheck to paycheck. We refuse to give our children and marriages over to the devil. We refuse to settle for nonproductive relationships for fear of being alone. The real key to us living full lives as kingdom representatives begins with a renewed mind according to the word and will of God.

Questions:
1. Write down the thoughts that passively go through your mind for at least one day. Are they in line with God's word?

2. Have you agreed with these thoughts?

3. If they are not in line with God's word, start the practice of rejecting them. Write down God's thought concerning them and meditate (think) on God's word and see those unproductive thoughts disappear and yourself transform.

Key Requirements for Transformation

**1. We must be mindful of our meditations.
Psalms 19:14 (KJV)** Let the words of my
mouth, and the meditation of my heart, be
acceptable in thy sight, O Lord, my strength,
and my redeemer.

**2. We must guard our gates: Portals of entry
both naturally and spiritually.**

> **Our eyes-** what we see
> **Our ears –** what we hear
> **Our mouths –** the words we speak
>
> **1 Corinthians 3:16 (KJV)** Know ye not that
> ye are the temple of God, and that the Spirit
> of God dwelleth in you?

3. We must know God's thoughts towards us.

Jeremiah 29:11 (KJV) For I know the
thoughts that I think toward you, saith the
Lord, thoughts of peace, and not of evil, to
give you an expected end.

Chapter 5
"Pressing Beyond Our Natural Limitations"
(Embracing our Authenticity)

When we are born, we are subjected to situations that are beyond our control. As human beings, we are instinctively inclined to protect what is near and dear to us. Although we are not always able to shield ourselves from the harmful effects that the changes of life bring, we must continue to press beyond all limiting conditions.

Have you ever been asked to do something yet, you felt you weren't equipped for the task? Have you ever compared yourself to others and even felt intimidated by their gifts and abilities? No matter who we are, no matter what our sphere of influence, there will come times in all of our lives when we will have feelings of inadequacy. The spirit of inadequacy is counted among the self-destructive tools that have the potential to limit our effectiveness in the kingdom. The feeling of inadequacy is the state or condition of being inadequate; it is insufficiency. When feelings of inadequacy are present, our progress is always limited.

The enemy wants to stop us at all cost, and he will do whatever, through whomever is willing to yield themselves to him. It comes as no surprise, when we see how many of our lives have been affected by people yielding themselves to be used of Satan and/or his demons. The one thing that we must be ever mindful of is, that these demons on assignment sometimes come disguised in ways that appeal to us. By appearance you think you have met your perfect match; this can come in the form of friendships, business connections, or even male female relationships. These individuals' actions and behaviors are a result of unaddressed issues of their past or present. We have often heard people talk about how wounded people wound others, and if we live long enough, we will cross paths with people that are walking casualties of mental, physical and, emotional wars. We encourage you to pay close attention to their behaviors in addition to your own. The very moment they are upset or can't have their way, there is an explosion. Many times, they will apologize and show remorse for their behavior but before long there is another outburst. It is far past time that we come to terms with the things that have attributed to limiting us from moving forward. We must also be mindful that in some instances, our limitations are self- imposed as a result of unmet expectations or poor choices. When we spend days, months, and even years believing God for something, the time of delay can be difficult. If we are honest with ourselves, our diminishing sense of hope can cause us to let our spiritual defenses down and we find ourselves compromising as a result of fear or desperation of seeing the manifestation of what we are hoping for. When this happens, we open the door to anger, rebellion, and pride. The time of delay can also make us feel as if God has forgotten us or that He doesn't love us. God created each of us for His purpose and He wants what's best for us. The one thing that God wants us to learn is how to trust that He knows what's best for us.

The Apostle Paul reminds us that we are God's workmanship created in the likeness and image of Christ. Not only are we created in His likeness and image, His love for us is beyond measure. Our mistakes and our weaknesses are no surprise to God. When we come to understand our true sonship and the power that dwells in us, we will also understand that our weaknesses make room for the might of God to kick in.

In Exodus 2:11- 3:22, Moses endured great process before being called by God to deliver the Children of Israel out of Egyptian bondage. In response to the call, Moses immediately began to offer excuses to God as to how he wasn't the one suitable for the job. The very things that Moses felt disqualified him for the assignment were minor to God and of course, He always had the solution.

It's Okay to Be Who God created you To Be

Each of us have gifts and talents that God has given us to share with others in one capacity or another. In order for us to be effective in our sharing, we must embrace our true authenticity. Then and only then, will the world see the power of God in action through us.

What is true Authenticity? Not false or copied; it is genuine, real having an origin unquestionable, it is representing one's true nature or beliefs; True to one's self.

When we are not ashamed of being all that we were created to be, it pleases the heart of God. As we align with the perfect will and plan of God, the people, the resources and the plan comes together as God intended. When reading further about the life of Moses, there is so much that we can all learn. Two things that come to mind are, our perspective and how we view things and the importance of obeying God's instructions. These two elements are vital keys to receiving all that God has promised. Yes, Moses was instrumental in helping to facilitate the deliverance of the children of Israel. He witnessed the many miraculous acts of God yet, his disobedience caused him to see the Promised Land without apprehending it.

Questions:
1. What's keeping you from receiving the promises of God?

2. Are you willing to do all that God requires of you?

3. Do you trust that God has your best interest at heart?

4. The time is at hand, are you ready to step out of   your comfort zone to advance the kingdom?

What God Requires of Us During the Press and Time of Trusting:

1. We must trust God and resist the urge to rely on our own strength.

Philippians 4:13 (KJV)
I can do all things through Christ which strengtheneth me.

2. **We must rid our minds of past negative experiences.**

   Isaiah 43:18 (KJV)
   Remember ye not the former things, neither consider the things
   of old.

3. **We must not dim our lights to appease others.**

   Matthew 5:16 (KJV)
   Let your light so shine before men, that they may see your good works, and glorify your Father which is in heaven.

4. **We must know that our image of ourselves determines our image of the God in us.**
   Proverbs 23:7 (a) (KJV) For as he thinketh in his heart, so is he:

5. **We must be a God pleaser and not a man pleaser.**

Acts 5:29 (b) (KJV) ......We ought to obey God rather than men.

Chapter 6
"Enduring the Process"

Life is filled with challenges and unexpected situations. It doesn't matter how good or righteous we think we are, there will come times in each of our lives when we are confronted with situations that cause is to question if we have done something wrong as a result of the difficult times that we have experienced.

Has God ever given you a dream or vision of something that He will do in your life? Certainly, most of us would say affirmatively yes in response to this question. When God gives us a dream or vision, He doesn't generally tell us the process that we will endure along the way. In the midst of waiting on the natural fulfillment of the promises of God, each of us will endure periods of processing and waiting on the timing of God. The word **time** is defined as the specific hour. **Process** is the method or series of actions to achieve results. What do you do when is seems like things are going opposite of what God promised? Periods of delay can often cause many emotions. During the times when our emotions are at a peak, we are tempted to throw in the towel. The enemy will do whatever he can to distract and discourage us. It is of utmost importance that we stay in prayer and, continually meditate the word because any wrong move can pose a threat to our assignment.

Walking in obedience during the Process

When God gives us specific instructions, we can't allow the disobedience of others to become a stumbling block for us. In Numbers the 20th chapter, when God told Moses to take the staff, gather the assembly together and speak to the rock to provide water for the people and livestock, Moses disobeyed the specific instructions of God. Not only did he strike the rock instead of speaking to it as God had instructed, Moses took credit for the miracle without letting the people know that God himself had performed the mighty act. When God allows us to lead in any capacity, we must not become so puffed up in pride that we do things that will grieve the heart of God. After all that Moses accomplished along the journey, he was able to see the Promised Land, but he was not able to enter in due to disobedience. **(See Numbers 20th Chapter)**

"When God Gives instruction"

Instinctively, we are inclined to act out of emotion. While this is a common practice among many of us, being emotionally led can pose a threat to our kingdom assignment. Most of us can relate to how it feels to anxiously wait for God to fulfill a promise.

In our moments of waiting, we place ourselves in compromising positions and often end up doing things that we later regret. It is not our responsibility to make the promise come to past. The one thing that we are obligated to do is to make sure that we are walking in obedience to God even when we don't fully understand.

Spirit vs. Emotions

One of the greatest indications that we are closer to receiving the promise, is revealed through increased pressure and spiritual warfare. Our ability to trust God and walking in faith is vital because by appearance, we are surrounded by opposition. During these times, we find ourselves questioning God and more than ever, it seems like God is silent. When God is silent, and we know we have done all that He has instructed us to do, we must continue to stand until He gives us further instructions.

Ephesians 6:13 (KJV) Wherefore take unto you the whole armor of God, that ye may be able to withstand in the evil day, and having done all, to stand.

Standing is not always easy to do; especially when it seems the odds are against us.

Faith and Obedience go Hand and Hand

When things appear opposite of what God has promised, it's easy to fall into a state of doubt and discouragement. We have to be careful that we are spiritually alert enough to discern what is taking place because walking by sight is one of Satan's greatest tool of distraction.

One of our greatest examples of faith and obedience is revealed through the life of our Lord and Savior Jesus Christ. Jesus was tempted by Satan, He was wrongly accused, there even came a time when He even felt forsaken by God, yet He pressed beyond his emotions and yielded His will, that the will of the Father might be done through Him. Not only did Jesus obey God, He kept the faith that God would fulfill His promise. **(See Matthew 26)**

Questions:

1. Are there moments in your life where you willfully rebelled against God's instructions or where you were connected to someone who was willfully disobedient to God's instructions? What was the result?

2. Write down the last set of instructions you believe God gave you. Are you doing them? If not, why? Pray about it, confess, and get back on track.

3. In what ways can you guard against being emotionally led, versus being led by the Holy Spirit.

4. Remind yourself of the inheritance you have received because of Jesus Christ's obedience to the Father. Who might be the beneficiary of your obedience?

Key Requirements for Walking in Obedience

1. **We must be willing to yield our will to the will of God.**

   Isaiah 1:19 (KJV) If you are willing and obedient, you will eat the good of the land

2. We must not allow what we see to distract us.

   2 Corinthians 5:7 (KJV) for we walk by faith and not by sight.

3. We must allow the word of God to be the final authority in our lives.

   Psalm 119:11(KJV) Thy word have I hid in my heart, that I might not sin against thee

4. We must endure the complete process knowing that the strength of God will enable us to do so.

   Philippians 4:13 (NKJV) I can do all things through Christ that strengthens me

Chapter 7
"Trusting God" (While We Wait)

One of the most difficult things for most of us is having the ability to wait on God to move in different areas of our lives. We have become so accustomed to having things how we want them and when we want them that we sometimes miss the beauty of going through the process. For the most part if we had our way, most of us would avoid going through our process due to fear of the unknown. In our quest to gain understanding and clarity as to why things happen the way they do, we have a natural tendency to become discouraged and weary when circumstances and situations seem to go opposite of what we were hoping for. When a loved one dies after and we have prayed and believed God for their healing, going through a bitter divorce despite of our attempts to come to a place of reconciliation are two common examples. A couple of additional examples are when there is confusion on the job and all you seek is peace, or when a physical illness lasts longer than expected when you know victory was won for you at Calvary. It is in the midst of these types of hardships that we tend to allow our emotions to get the best of us. When we spend most of our time talking about our problems, our attention shifts, causing us to become consumed with our go through rather focusing our attention on all that God has promised. There are times in all of our lives when we have to wait. In our time of waiting, we must maintain an attitude of expectancy. One of the greatest examples of waiting with expectancy is revealed in the life of the woman with the issue of blood as recorded in (**Matthew 9:20-22**) In reading the text, we find a woman with an issue of blood that arrested the attention of Jesus. One can only imagine the pain this woman must have felt being an outcast for 12 long years. According to Hebrew law, this woman was not even allowed to touch another person because she was considered unclean, just like the leper and demon possessed man, she was unclean. For 12 years, this woman couldn't live a normal life.... She couldn't go out to eat with her friends, she couldn't go to the salon to get her hair and nails done, she couldn't go to the movies to watch the latest show. After all, she was unclean. One can only imagine that after all those years of suffering at one point or another, this woman must have become weary and she must have even felt frustrated and even depressed. She spent all she had trying to get rid of her issue, trying to get rid of her debilitating disease that kept her isolated from others. This woman was not someone who spent her time looking to see what Jesus was doing for others like some of us. This woman had become desperate enough to position herself in the crowd where she could receive her healing. Are you desperate enough to press your way to get what you need from God? Are you willing to wait for the optimal time to step out of your comfort zone? The woman with the issue of blood stepped out against the odds to receive what she needed from Jesus. In this hour we have got to press beyond all natural and emotional limitations. This woman could have given up after exhausting all her natural resources, yet there was a determination on the inside of her that would not allow her to give up. When we know that what God has promised us something, no matter how long it may seem, we must trust God while we wait.

Questions:

1. Are you trusting God while you wait?

2. Write down personal transformations or situations that you've needed help in?

3. Have you been passively waiting or aggressively pursuing Jesus in these areas?

<u>Key Requirements While Waiting</u>

1. We must pray in the spirit continually.
   Ephesians 6:18 (KJV) Praying always with all prayer and supplication in the Spirit, and watching thereunto with all perseverance and supplication for all saints;

2. We must trust that God is able to exceed our expectations.
Ephesians 3:20 (KJV)
Now unto him that is able to do exceeding abundantly above all that we could ever ask or think, according to the power that worketh in us,

3. Our faith must remain active.
Hebrews 11:1 (KJV) Now faith is the substance of things hoped for, the evidence of things not seen.
4. We must exercise our kingdom authority by speaking the word of God over our lives.

Isaiah 55:11 (KJV) so shall my word be that goeth forth out of my mouth: it shall not return unto me void, but it shall accomplish that which I please, and it shall prosper in the thing whereto I sent it.

Chapter 8
"Maintaining Our Focus" (Beyond the Distractions)

Throughout the word of God, we see many examples of people that stood on God's word even when conditions didn't appear to be favorable. Has God ever given you a promise yet, when you looked at your circumstances things looked opposite of what God said? As the divine purpose and plan of God begins to unfold in our lives, there will be times when we are confronted with distractions.

What are distractions?

Distractions – that which distracts or divides our attention or prevents concentration. (Ex. Financial problems, relationship issues, drama on the job, health problems, poor living conditions.)

When we continue to allow ourselves to dwell on the things that are causing our attention to be divided, our lack of concentration can hinder our progress. When something has been identified as a distraction, it is vitally important that we make every effort to press beyond what appears to be happening in the natural and by faith, we must keep our focus on the promise.

Distractions vs. Faith

During the times of distraction, our faith will be tried and tested.

No matter how difficult the trial or test, we must trust that God is faithful to do what He promised.

Hebrews 11:6 (KJV) but without faith it is impossible to please Him: for he that cometh to Him must first believe that he is and that He is a rewarder to them that diligently seek Him.
What does it mean to be diligent?

Diligent- Steady in application to business, constant in effort or exertion to accomplish what is under taken assiduous, attentive, industrious not idle or negligent **(KJV Bible Dictionary)**

One of the greatest examples of diligence in the midst of distractions is revealed through the life of young Joseph. When we look at the life of Joseph as recorded in the 37th chapter of Genesis, we see a depiction of Joseph whose name means increaser or adder. Joseph was the son of Rachel and Jacob and was born when Jacob was around 91 years old. It is believed that Joseph was his father's favorite because he was conceived in his father's old age. To many, Joseph was known for his prophetic dreams and, his coat of many colors which was given to him by his father. Customarily, when fathers gave certain garments to their sons, it was symbolic of passing on the mantle of blessings. As the story of the life Of Joseph unfolds, we see a disturbing account of how Joseph shared his God given prophetic dream with his family and because of their jealousy, Joseph's brothers plotted to kill him. Later we discover that the older brother Ruben talked his brothers into throwing Joseph into a pit instead. One can only imagine how painful it must have been for Joseph to absorb the harsh reality of being betrayed by his brothers. The story goes on to tell us that Joseph went from the pit, to being sold into slavery, later he was put in prison for false accusations.

Processed for Purpose

Never in a million years could Joseph have imagined the process and number of distractions that he would encounter when God gave him the prophetic promise. As we reflect upon our lives and the many trials that we have had to face during our times of waiting on the fulfillment of the promises of God, many of us would agree that the process was filled with distractions. The story goes on to tell us that after enduring the devastation of being betrayed and falsely accused, Joseph's God given the interpretation of Pharaoh's dream helped Pharaoh and the Egyptians to avoid 7 years of famine. Pharaoh was so grateful for Joseph's wisdom that he made Joseph second ruler in command Of Egypt. When all was said and done, Joseph was able to be a blessing to his family. He was able to forgive the people that betrayed him, and he was able to acknowledge the fact that even in the midst of distractions, the hand of God was with Him leading and guiding his every step.

Temptations Along the Journey

In reading the text of the life of Joseph, we never hear any mention of Joseph showing any signs of wanting to quit yet, the pressures of life can often make us feel as if there is no hope. What do you do when God has spoken a word over your life and things don't appear to be coming together? What do you do when the pressure is really intense, and God is silent? It is in the midst of our moments of uncertainty that we are impelled to seek the heart of God like never before. It is in our seeking that God begins to reveal His many attributes to us causing us to come to know Him in a better way. When our head knowledge becomes heart knowledge, the power of God becomes real in our lives. This power not only transforms our lives, but we are empowered to do great exploits in the earth.

Daniel 11:32b (KJV) but the people that do know their God shall be strong and do exploits.

What does it mean to know?

Know - To perceive with certainty to understand clearly to have a clear and certain perception of truth, fact, or anything that actually exists. **(KJV Bible Dictionary)**

Just as Joseph learned to trust the process even during difficult times, it is the will and heart of God for each of us to do the same.

Questions:

1. What distractions have you faced thus far on your journey?
2. Have you encountered betrayal, false accusation, etc. because of a promise you received from God? Read the end of Joseph's story to see how he handled it.
3. Are you seeking to know God in a deeper way?

Key Requirements for Pressing Beyond Distractions:

1. **We must keep the vision in mind.**
   Habakkuk 2:3 (KJV) For the vision is yet for an appointed time, but at the end it shall speak, and not lie: though it tarry, wait for it; because it will surely come, it will not tarry.

2. **We must not be emotionally led but, spirit led.**
   Romans 8:14 (KJV) For as many as are led by the spirit of God, they are the sons of God.

3. We must release and forgive often.

Luke 17:3-4 Take heed to yourselves: if thy brother trespasses against thee, rebuke him; and if he repent, forgive him. Vs.4 And if he trespasses against you three seven times in a day, and seven times in a day turn again to thee, saying I repent; thou shall forgive him.

4. We must seek Godly counsel concerning the promise, not man.

Psalms 1:1 (KJV) Blessed is the man that walketh not in the counsel of the ungodly, nor standeth in the way of sinners, nor sitteth in the seat of the scornful.

Chapter 9

"Releasing the Weight of Anxiety"

Philippians 4:6-7(KJV) be careful for nothing; but in everything by prayer and supplication with thanksgiving let your requests be made known unto God. And the peace of God, which passeth all understanding, shall keep your hearts and minds through Christ Jesus.

The one thing that all of us are guilty of is falling prey to the emotion of anxiety/worry. Seeing all the things that are going on around us, having to experience the effects of dealing with the stressors of everyday life, our natural tendency is to focus our attention on our problems. Everybody has problems. Many times, we indulge in unfruitful conversations not realizing that when we actively participate in negative conversations, we are unconsciously taking a stance or position of pessimism. God wants us to be mindful of the words that we speak because our words have the power to create. You see, because we were created in the likeness and image of God our words have power. It is through the creative power of words that our world was formed; therefore, when we are conscious of the words that we speak, we are more apt to take an optimistic view on things. One thing that is vital in our Christian walk is having the faith to call those things that are not as though they are. That means I may be sick in my body, but my confession is, "Jesus has already paid the price for my healing". I may be struggling financially but, "Jesus promised to supply all my needs". There may be confusion at home, on the job and even in my relationship but God promised to keep me in perfect peace if I keep my mind on Him.

When we look at our focal scripture, we find that the Apostle Paul was experiencing a great number of things that could have easily caused him to become anxious. The people at Philippi were at odds with one another, the preachers in Rome were filled with envy and strife and they were out to get Paul according to **Philippians 1:15**. To make matters worse, Paul was in prison awaiting trial and possible execution. In the midst of these trying circumstances, the one word that was repeated throughout this Epistle was, word rejoice!!! According to the King James Bible Dictionary, to **rejoice** means to experience joy and gladness in a high degree. It means to be exhilarated with lively and pleasurable sensations. It means to exult.

When we relate our text to our daily lives, just as Paul was able to rejoice in adversity, God wants us to rejoice in adversity as well. When we look at **Philippians 4th chapter in verses 6-7**, Paul's example shows us how we can overcome anxiety/worry. The word anxious in the Greek means to be pulled in different directions. (Example is wrestling between faith and doubt) The synonym for anxiety is worry which comes from the word struggle.

From the natural point of view, anxiety/worry has been said to cause physical problems such as headaches, neck/back pain, and high blood pressure. It can cause ulcers, has the ability to affect the digestive system I and effects our coordination and our ability to think clearly.

From a spiritual point of view, anxiety/worry about people, material things and circumstances can rob us of our peace. When we are consumed with negative emotions, we end up **self-destructing** simply because we have mentally made the decision that we are going to believe the report of the enemy. It is our responsibility to make the decision to replace wrong thoughts with the word of God.

Psalms 19: 14 (KJV)

Let the words of my mouth, and the meditation of my heart, be acceptable in thy sight, O Lord, my strength, and my redeemer.

To **let** means to allow or permit, it means allow occupancy or use of.

That means that when we allow wrong thoughts to linger in our minds, it is an act of our own will. God wants us to replace our anxieties with worship. In **Psalms 34:1 (KJV)**, the writer says: I will bless the Lord at all times: His praise shall continually be in my mouth. No matter what it looks like, no matter what it feels like, I'm determined to bless Him anyhow... The word of God teaches us that being anxious/worrying is a sin. In the Sermon on the Mount, Jesus made it clear that anxiety comes from a lack of faith.

Hebrews 11:6 declares, but without faith it's impossible to please Him: for He that comes to God must first believe that He is and that He is a rewarder to them that diligently seek Him. When there is a diligent seek in us, Kingdom is our main priority. That's why Jesus admonishes us in **Matthew 6:33** to seek first the kingdom of God and His righteousness and all things will be added unto you.

Questions:

1. Write down your anxieties and pray about them.
2. Are you seeking the kingdom of God?

Keys to Overcoming Anxiety/Worry

1. Pray about everything understanding and taking confidence in the fact that God is able to handle all of our problems.

2. With prayer and supplication we must openly and honestly pray with expectancy placing a demand on the anointing of God until we get results.

3. We must pray with thanksgiving thanking God in advance, letting Him know how much we appreciate His love and merciful kindness.

4.   The end result is the reward of peace. When we rid our hearts/minds of emotional anxiety, God promises to give us peace that surpasses all understanding that will guard our hearts and minds through Christ Jesus.

There will be many days when we will face trials and difficult situations, but we must trust that our God is in control. Things may look opposite of what He showed us yet, we must be determined not to worry. In the midst of the storm, in the midst of persecution, we must determine that were going to wait on God....

Chapter 10
"Walking into Purpose" (Keeping Hope Alive)

Romans 8:28 (KJV)

And we know that all things work together for good to them that love God, to them who are called according to His purpose.

When we look at the way time and life circumstances change from day to day, many of us are experiencing a sense of urgency in our spirits as it relates to getting into proper alignment and position concerning God's will for our lives. For some of us, we have endured trying times in our finances, our relationships, in our health and so many other areas yet we have an assurance on the inside giving us hope that everything will be alright. The circumstances and situations we have encountered have in many instances been sent to either distract us or to build our spiritual stamina. Nonetheless, we are reminded that all things work together for good to those that love God, to those that are called according to His purpose. It's time to get on purpose…

The dictionary defines **purpose** as the reason for which something is done or created. It is the reason for which something exists. There is a purpose for everything there is, an appointed time for which we are destined to walk into our purpose. The time is at hand… The word **time** is defined as the specific hour.

Ecclesiastes 3:1-8 there is a time for everything and season for every activity under the heavens. A time to be born and a time to die, a time to plant and a time to uproot, a time to kill and a time to heal, a time to tear down and a time to build , a time to weep and a time to laugh, a time to mourn and a time to dance ,a time to scatter stones and a time to gather them, a time to embrace and a time to refrain , a time to search and a time to give up, a time to keep and a time to throw away, a time to be silent and a time to speak, a time to love and a time to hate, a time of war and a time of peace.

These verses express how important timing is and the key or secret to peace with God is discovering, accepting and appreciating God's perfect timing. The dangers of doubting and resenting God's timing can lead to despair, rebellion and moving ahead of God, leaning to our own understanding. Can you recall an instance or situation where you moved and got ahead of God and got negative results? Even in those not so pleasant experiences, things always seem to work together for our good. Things work together for our good even when we experience difficulties as part of living in a fallen world. Had we not experienced being violated as a child, or being raised in a single parent home, had we not experienced rejection from our peers , had we not experienced church hurt, had we not experienced being admitted to the mental hospital for depression, had we not experienced the loss of a loved one or the bitter divorce, had we not experienced the loss of a house or car, had we not experienced abuse at the hands of someone who said they loved us, had we not experienced the betrayal of a so called friend, or the loss of a job, had we not experienced being addicted to drugs or alcohol, had we not experienced going to jail, or being raped we may not have come to know God as the one who triumphs over these things, or have the compassion to help others that have experienced the same ills. Had we not experienced being healed of an infirmity then we wouldn't be able to minister to others that face the same issues. Our key scripture explains how God works all things together for our good, not just isolated incidents. That doesn't mean that everything that happens to us is good because evil is always present in our fallen world, but God is able to turn every situation around for our long range good. God isn't working to make us happy, but He desires for us to fulfill His purpose in the earth. Are you on purpose?

Keeping Hope Alive

Proverbs 13:12 (KJV)
Hope deferred maketh the heart sick: but when desire cometh, it is a tree of life.

The journey to walking in purpose can be difficult. As people of God, many times we allow ourselves to rehearse the problem as opposed to trusting the God of the problem. In our key scripture, when preparing   his son for the throne, Solomon taught the wisdom of keeping citizens filled with hope in an effort to keep them from becoming discouraged. When we relate our scripture to our current day experiences, over a period of time, we come to realize that we don't always receive things immediately. There are times in all of our lives when we have to wait and waiting can be really difficult. It is in the midst of our waiting that we tend to develop a feeling of hopelessness. Hopelessness is said to be one of the most destructive and painful feelings of the human experience. We're living in this world of constant change, we see so many things happening all around us. Life experiences and personal disappointments have a way of causing us to feel like we will never receive the things that we are hoping for.

We hope for healing in our bodies.

We hope for peace and restoration in our families.

We hope for that dream house or car.

We hope for the right career and financial stability.

We hope for the salvation of our loved ones.

We hope for the coming together and uniting with the man or woman that God has ordained for us.

No matter who we are and no matter what our position or title, in one area or another, each of us is hoping for something.

The dictionary defines the word **Hope** as a feeling of expectation and desire for a certain thing to happen. It is a person or thing in which expectations are centered. It is the feeling that what is wanted can be had. The King James Version of the bible uses the word hope 133 times (44) in the Old Testament (89) in the New Testament. When hope is deferred, it is postponed or delayed. It is suspended or withheld for a certain time or event. As human beings, we can live 40 days without food, 3 days without water, about 8 minutes without air, but can you believe that we can't go a second without hope? When we look at our key scripture, clause (A) says, hope deferred maketh the heart sick. We know that the word of God uses the word heart and mind interchangeably so when referring to the heart, the writer is not talking about our blood pumping organ, he is actually talking about the mind which is made up of the mind, will, emotions and the intellect of man.

When there is a delay in hope, it can be very painful to the mind. By nature, we have a tendency to allow ourselves to become consumed with receiving the things according to our time clock. The two things that lie between hope and desire are process and time.

Process is the method or series of actions to achieve results.

The one thing that we often miss out on is the complete details of what the process entails. When God gives us a dream or vision, he never tells us what we will go through. In the midst of the process, we will have distractions, those unexpected occurrences that have way of draining us physically and emotionally such as an unexpected death, the loss of a job, relationship or health issues. It is during the process, we may encounter seducing spirits that will try to cause us to regress into sinful behavior that we once indulged in. (When I would do good, evil was always present.) During the process, our character is developed. As God begins to show us our personal flaws, we must take the necessary steps to improve in those areas. It is during the process, we endure disappointment, rejection, and persecution. It is during the process, that we experience heartache and heartbreak. It is during the process that we come to realize we can't put our trust in man. It is during the process that we learn to release and forgive. The time of processing doesn't always look good and it doesn't always feel good, but we have to trust that it's working together for our good.

When we look at the (B) clause of our key scripture, it says when desire cometh, it is a tree of life.

When, speaks of the time which is, the specific hour. When the hour or time is at hand, we can't rely on our senses as the indicator for what God is doing. The reality of the matter is, fact and truth can conflict with one another, therefore relying on our senses can cause us to miss God. The fact may say, "I have no money in the bank.", but the truth says, "I'm the lender and not the borrower."

The fact may say, "They are talking about me and scandalizing my name, but the truth says, "No weapon formed against me shall prosper."

The fact may say, "I'm feeling oppressed and depressed." but, the truth says, "He will keep me in perfect peace if I keep my mind on Him."

The fact may say "Fear and intimidation are trying to consume me.", but the truth says, "God has not given me the spirit of fear but of power, love and of sound mind. "The fact may say, Pain and sickness is attacking my body but, the truth says, "He was wounded for my transgressions, He was bruised for my iniquities, the chastisement of my peace was upon Him and with His stripes, I am healed.

Questions:

1. Are there specific incidents that have happened in your life that appear to be opposing you and the fulfillment of your purpose in the earth? If so, write them down. Ask the Holy Spirit to give you a revelation of how these things are working together for your good.

2. Write down a few practical things you can do to keep hope alive.

3. Where do you feel you are as it relates to the timing of God and the divine purpose that He has for your life?

Key requirements For Enduring

1. We must refocus our attention on God.
Psalm 121:1-2
I will lift up my eyes unto the hills, from whence cometh my help. My help cometh from the Lord, which made heaven and earth.

2. We must bless the Lord no matter how we feel.
Psalm 103: 1-2 (KJV)
Bless the Lord, O my soul: and all that is within me, bless His holy name. Bless the Lord, O my soul and forget not all His benefits:

3. We must endure hardness as a good soldier.
2 Timothy 2:3-4
You therefore must endure hardship as a good soldier of Jesus Christ. No one entangled in warfare entangles himself with the affairs of this life, that he may please him who enlisted him as a soldier.

Parting Thoughts

There is so much that God desires to do in the lives of His people. As long as there is breath in our bodied, we have the ability to choose the path that we want to take. Are you willing to release unnecessary weights to run the race that that is set before you? The time has come , the kingdom is at hand... Are you ready to lose weight?